let's go NUTS!

SEEDS WE EAT

by april pulley sayre

Beach Lane Books

New York   London   Toronto   Sydney   New Delhi

For my grandmother,
who took her eighth grade ag students to meet
the great seed hero, George Washington Carver, in his lab.

A cashew thank-you to Andrea Welch, Allyn Johnston, and Lauren Rille for helping these books sing. Gini and Gene Bamber of Bamber's Superette, I so appreciate your help! My gratitude, as always, to the South Bend Farmer's Market folks (Marie!). A special thanks to the following farmer's market vendors, whose seeds were photographed for this book, though not all were ultimately used: Hovenkamp's Produce, Vite's Produce, Johnson's Produce, Coffee and Tea Thyme, Sweet Street, Maple Land Farms. Thank you also to these folks who allowed me to photograph: Saigon Market, the University of Notre Dame South Dining Hall, El Paraiso, Down to Earth Natural Foods, the Purple Porch Co-op, and the Aurora Seed and Feed Store. Thank you to Isabel, the Reshock Family, and Michael, Patti, and Ken. Thanks to the math crew: Margaret, Amanda, Cheryl, and Linda. Lifetime supply of native pecans to Jeff for helping me seed wrangle and set up photos. My apologies to all my friends and relatives who have been subjected to seed-related jokes, puns, recipes, and factoids. Expect this to continue.

"What shall I learn of beans or beans of me? I cherish them, I hoe them, early and late
I have an eye to them; and this is my day's work. It is a fine broad leaf to look on."
—Henry David Thoreau, from his chapter "The Bean Field" in his book *Walden*

BEACH LANE BOOKS • An imprint of Simon & Schuster Children's Publishing Division • 1230 Avenue of the Americas, New York, New York 10020 • Copyright © 2013 by April Pulley Sayre • All rights reserved, including the right of reproduction in whole or in part in any form. • BEACH LANE BOOKS is a trademark of Simon & Schuster, Inc. • For information about special discounts for bulk purchases, please contact Simon & Schuster Special Sales at 1-866-506-1949 or business@simonandschuster.com. • The Simon & Schuster Speakers Bureau can bring authors to your live event. For more information or to book an event, contact the Simon & Schuster Speakers Bureau at 1-866-248-3049 or visit our website at www.simonspeakers.com. • Book design by Lauren Rille • The text for this book is set in Calvert. • Manufactured in China • 0613 SCP • First Edition • 10 9 8 7 6 5 4 3 2 1 • Library of Congress Cataloging-in-Publication Data • Sayre, April Pulley. • Let's go nuts! / by April Pulley Sayre.—First edition. • p. cm. • ISBN 978-1-4424-6728-6 (hardcover) • ISBN 978-1-4424-6727-9 (eBook) • 1. Nuts—Juvenile literature. 2. Beans—Juvenile literature. 3. Grain—Juvenile literature. 4. Seeds—Juvenile literature. I. Title. • SB401.A4S28 2013 • 641.3'45—dc23 • 2012040661

Bravo, black beans!
Rah, rah, rice!

Seeds are meals.
They're snacks. They spice!

Love a legume?
Lentils—yum!

Chickpeas, split peas.
Fill your tum!

Kidney. Lima.
Pinks and whites.

**Soybeans. Mung beans—
zesty bites!**

Friend a fava.
Pintos? Please!

Anasazi.
Black-eyed peas.

Nod for navy.
Runners. Red.

Bean there. Look out—
nuts ahead!

Hickory. Hazelnut.
Coconut's here!

All for almonds?
Chestnut cheer!

Brazil nut. Butternut. Walnut wave!

Mmmm...macadamia!
Pecan's a fave.

Peanut, pine nut.
Go, nuts, go!

Chew cashew— or pistachio!

Greet your grains.
Hi, rye! Hi, wheat!

**Boats of oats
and corn to eat.**

Keen for quinoa?
Wild for rice.

Buckwheat. Barley.
Time to spice!

Open, sesame!
Dill's ahead.

Human? Try cumin.
Or mustard, instead!

Vie for vanilla.
Nutmeg, now!

Cardamom. Coriander.
Carob, cacao!

Beans, grains, spices. Nuts fill needs.
Shell them. Share them!

Celebrate

seeds!

A Few More Handfuls:
The Scoop on Seeds

Are nuts, beans, and grains really seeds?

Yes. Plant an unshelled almond and it can grow to become an almond tree. Plant an uncooked kidney bean and it can grow to become a low, bushy plant or climbing vine. Plant a grain of wheat and it can become a slender grass that leans in the wind. All nuts, beans, and grains are seeds.

Many spices, which we use to flavor food, are seeds too. A dill seed can grow to become a tall, feathery-leaved plant. (Some spices aren't seeds: they are flowers, bark, or other plant parts. Herbs, which also flavor food, are leaves.) Seeds are a major part of what people eat worldwide.

Why are seeds such good food?

Seeds are power packs of nutrition. They contain a plant embryo—the beginning of a young plant. But they also contain energy, stored as plant food. This energy will power the young plant until it forms green leaves. (Once it has leaves, a young plant can make food for itself through photosynthesis.) A seed's energy is stored in the form of fats, proteins, and starches. That makes seeds nutritious and tasty. Seeds are also an excellent food because they store well. In nature, a seed may need to wait until rains come or the weather is warm enough to grow. Some seeds spoil after a year. Others can last for decades. (In Israel, a two-thousand-year-old seed from a date palm tree was sprouted and the tree is growing well!) Their durability makes seeds a good food to store to eat in winter, during droughts, and any other time when people must wait until the next harvest.

Eat them or plant them?

Are the seeds we eat the same kind of seeds we plant? Yes. A dried lima bean you buy to eat can also be planted. (Beans in a can, already cooked, will not grow.) Farm stores sell seeds for growing, not eating. These are the same kinds of seeds we eat. But some have been coated with bacteria to help them grow or chemicals to discourage pests. Seeds meant for planting should not be eaten in case they have been treated in these ways.

Why don't seeds we eat grow inside our stomachs?

The human digestive tract, with its churning acid and food moving through, is not a good place for plants to grow. Most large seeds we eat are broken apart by our teeth when we chew. They are broken down further by digestive juices in our stomach and intestines. Your body processes the fats, starches, and proteins and takes energy from them. The energy in the seed powers you in much the way it powers a young plant.

But what if a seed is not broken down by all this crunching, crushing, and chemical work? That's okay. These seeds are just passing through. They will end up in your feces—your poop. In nature, some seeds are spread this way. They sprout in the droppings of animals that have eaten them. The rest of the dropping becomes fertilizer for the young plant.

Nut or not?

A nut is a single large edible seed inside a hard shell. Typically, nuts grow on trees. Nuts are full of oil, protein, fiber, vitamins, and minerals. The oil in nuts makes them creamy, tasty, and rich in calories.

Peanuts don't grow on trees or have a hard shell. Peanuts are actually beans. They are grouped with nuts because they are used in a similar way in cooking. Quite a few seeds that cooks call nuts wouldn't actually fit the definition of true nuts according to botanists—scientists who study plants.

The world's largest edible nut, the coconut, grows on coconut palm trees. Wind and waves carry coconuts from one island to the next. If they reach sand and soil, they can root and grow into new trees.

Nut allergies

Some people are allergic to peanuts or other nuts. That means their bodies misidentify these foods as "enemies" and react too strongly to their presence. Nut allergy symptoms may include a rash, tingling tongue, throat swelling, or difficulty breathing. These symptoms may go away after a few minutes but then return, much more seriously, a few hours later. Severe reactions can be life-threatening.

People with these allergies may need to avoid certain nuts entirely. Yet a recent study showed that children and adults, even those with family members who have nut allergies, are not good at identifying nuts. Doctors are calling for us to read food labels and to know which nut is which—in all its forms: boiled, roasted, in the shell, and shelled. By getting to know nuts, we can help our family members, classmates, and friends with nut allergies stay safe and healthy.

Bring on the beans!

Beans are members of the legume (LEG-yoom) family. Their seeds form inside pods. A pod isn't generally as hard as a nut shell. There are two or more beans in a pod. Unlike nuts, which mostly grow on trees, edible beans tend to grow on vines or small, low-growing plants.

Beans are very nutritious. They are full of protein, starch, and vitamins. Many of the beans in this book are in their dried form. Beans can be stored this way for a long time. To prepare them, some must be soaked in water for a while, even overnight, until they become plump. This softens them for cooking.

Beans aren't just good for the human body—they're good for the soil. Legumes tend to make the soil better for later crops grown in the same field. Legumes help capture nitrogen from the air and convert it to a form other plants can use.

Cacao or cocoa?

Chocolate is made from cacao (kuh-KOW) beans that grow in pods on trees native to Central and South America. Fresh cacao seeds, covered in gooey white pulp, are scooped out of the pod. They are laid out to ferment and dry; then they are roasted. Later the beans are ground up to make cocoa. Cacao, the name of the bean, is pronounced and spelled differently from cocoa, (KOH-KOH), the dried chocolate powder used in cakes, brownies, and hot chocolate.

Go, go, grains!

Grains, also called cereals, are edible seeds of the grass family. Grains don't grow in hard shells, like nuts do. They don't form in pods, as most beans do. Their seeds, or kernels, are grown on grass stalks.

Most species of rice originated in Asia. However, wild rice, with its thin, dark grains, is not closely related to Asian rices. A traditional food of Native Americans, wild rice is harvested from wetlands in the Great Lakes region of North America.

Like rice, corn is an ancient plant and has been grown for at least ten thousand years. Sweet corn is the soft type people eat off corncobs. Popcorn is a kind of corn that has a very hard outer covering. Tiny pockets of moisture inside the popcorn form steam when heated and explode outward, "popping" the kernel.

Wheat, rice, and corn are the most widely grown grains. But there are others, too, such as barley, rye, oats, millet, fonio, sorghum, teff, and triticale. Buckwheat, amaranth, and quinoa are seeds, but not in the grass family. In cooking, these tiny seeds are treated as grains because their use is so similar.

Seeds in cookpots and cultures

People all over the world have found ways to change seeds' textures and tastes for use in meals. Alfalfa beans, mung beans, broccoli seeds, soybeans, and radish seeds tossed in soups, sandwiches, and stir-fries are often sprouted before they are eaten. Soy sauce, miso, doenjang, and other sauces used in Asian food are made from fermented beans and grains. Below are some more kinds of seeds that we change before they are eaten.

Seeds for spreads, breads, and noodles

Seeds are often ground up or mashed to make delicious foods. Ground sesame seeds (called tahini) and mashed chickpeas are the main ingredients in hummus. Peanuts are ground to become peanut butter. Flour, the white or brownish powder used to make breads and noodles, is made from ground-up seeds. Which seeds? It varies! Wheat bread. Rye bread. Buckwheat pancakes. Lots of different grains can be used. The thin Indian crepes called dosas are made from rice flour and ground lentil-like beans called urad. The clear, glasslike noodles used in slurpable Asian soups are typically made from rice or mung beans.

Seeds we drink

Soy milk, rice milk, coconut milk, and almond milk are made from soaked, ground, and sometimes cooked seeds. (Coconut water, unlike coconut milk, occurs naturally in young green coconuts. As the coconut matures, the liquid evaporates, leaving behind more and more of the white "meat" we think of as coconut.) Tofu is made from soy milk that is curdled. The process is similar to the way cheese is made from curdled cow's milk, goat's milk, or sheep's milk.

Seeing the world through seeds

Dive into seeds and you'll find not just tasty food, but connections to many cultures and continents. Lima beans, for instance, draw their name from Lima, the capital of Peru. For more than fifteen hundred years, black-eyed peas have been a lucky food eaten during Rosh Hashanah, the Jewish New Year. Aztecs used cacao beans as a form of money! Even language has beans in it. Lenses—curved pieces of glass such those in eyeglasses—draw their name from the shape of a lentil bean. Take a closer look at the seeds in gardens, on branches, on your plate, and on store shelves. You may find a bit of science and history waiting.

For a key to identifying the seeds in this book and a bibliography of seed resources, including cookbooks, children's books, and food science books related to seeds we eat, visit AprilSayre.com.